A gift for

From

Published in 2010 by Helen Exley Giftbooks in Great Britain.

12 11 10 9 8 7 6 5 4 3 2 1

Selection and arrangement copyright © Helen Exley 2010.
IMPORTANT COPYRIGHT NOTICE: Pam Brown and Dalton Harold © Helen Exley 2010.
The moral right of the author has been asserted.

ISBN: 978-1-84634-538-8

EDITED BY DALTON EXLEY.
Photographs by Richard Exley and from The Garden Collection.

With special thanks to Liz and Elaine at The Garden Collection for all of their help on my project.

Helen Exley Giftbooks, 16 Chalk Hill, Watford, WD19 4BG, UK.
www.helenexleygiftbooks.com

My Garden

...my little piece of heaven

EDITED BY DALTON EXLEY

Spheres of fire, of rock, of ice.

Gigantic burning suns and barren moons.

And only we have snowdrops in the spring

and sparrows in the hedge

and apple trees.

This is a garden, set in a wilderness of stars.

We need to cherish it.

PAM BROWN, B.1928

Green shoots in the spring
are nothing short of miraculous.
They are truly my life
support machine.

BARNEY BARDSLEY,
FROM "A HANDFUL OF EARTH"

I can't conceive of a person observing
a beautiful garden and not being somehow
moved or touched. I know that I immediately
begin to unwind in a garden.
My internal clock slows down.
I think gardens probably have that effect on everybody,
whether they are conscious of the change
or not and whether they're gardeners or not.
That's part of what's so magical
about a garden.

FROM "TENDING THE EARTH, MENDING THE SPIRIT"

A GARDEN IS A CANVAS TO BE EMBROIDERED YEAR AFTER YEAR.

PAM BROWN, B.1928

He who plants
a garden
plants happiness.

CHINESE PROVERB

…my garden teaches me that everything takes time,
that sometimes there's nothing wrong
with being slow and methodical. I can't find
a better prescription at any drugstore.

MELISSA, IN "TENDING THE EARTH, MENDING THE SPIRIT"

A garden...is the purest of human pleasures;
it is the greatest refreshment to the spirit
of man, without which buildings and palaces
are but gross handiworks.

FRANCIS BACON (1561-1626)

If you want to be happy
for a short time,
get drunk;
happy for a long time,
fall in love;
happy forever,
take up gardening.

CHINESE SAYING

A garden
is the microcosm
of our lives
– a constant changing,
a constant loss,
– a constant creation.
Always a new wonder.
Always a new hope.

PAM BROWN, B.1928

I f you garden then you are immediately
at the heart of a great mystery that will unfold
new revelations for the rest of your days.

MONTY DON, B.1955, FROM "MY ROOTS"

The garden is a place
of private communion.
It's very deep; it's very secret.
One has a sense of presence
beyond one's immediate
surroundings.
The religion of a garden is
between yourself and
the universe, with all its
eternal mysteries.

STANLEY KUNITZ

Gardening is part of my search for inner peace, because I really do feel at one with the plants that I'm tending. It's such a peaceful, beautiful, and natural thing to do.

JONATHON, IN "TENDING THE EARTH, MENDING THE SPIRIT"

Someone who loves a garden, gets to enjoy
a slice of simpler living, and the peace that this
brings, which no one can ever put a price on.

DALTON HAROLD

When you bury your nose in a beautiful rose,
the heart can't help but lift.

ESTHER RANTZEN

When there's new growth bursting out all over,
everything fresh, green, and flourishing,
the plants are little rockets of success going off....

JACQUELINE HERITEAU

A part of your heart and mind and spirit
goes into the making of a garden.
It is as if something of yourself grew and blossomed there.

PAM BROWN, B.1928

What is paradise? But a garden,
an orchard of trees and herbs full of pleasure
and nothing there but delights.

WILLIAM LAWSON

Gardens are places where we can connect
with the weather, the seasons and the natural
rhythms of plants and animals.

MONTY DON, B.1955

Here in the house is light
and heat at command,
sounds and stories of our choice.
A closed world. But there,
only a pane of glass away
is the universe,
is the scent of grass.

PAM BROWN, B.1928

We are living in a very sterile, artificial world,
almost totally removed from nature.
As I walk through big cities,
I see the concrete-and-steel environment
that people are cooped up in all day long.
Plants put us back in touch with the natural world
that we come from.
Even if it's unconscious, people feel a need for
more than papers, computers, and TV.
Something as simple as walking into a garden
can help meet that need within us.

FROM "TENDING THE EARTH, MENDING THE SPIRIT"

No one can deny the possibility of magic
if they have a garden.

PAM BROWN, B.1928

One of the great things about gardening
is that when the huge wave of summer
does finally break, and its leaping curve
of green flings into every garden
a marvellous iridescent spray of petals,
in colours our language hasn't caught up
with yet, its joyful and indiscriminate tide
lifts everyone off their feet - both proper
gardeners and people like me.

PAUL JENNINGS

That we find a crystal or a poppy
beautiful means that we are less alone,
that we are more deeply
inserted into existence than the course
of a single life
would lead us to believe.

JOHN BERGER, FROM "THE SENSE OF SIGHT"

When at last I took the time
to look into the heart of a flower,
it opened up a whole new world –
a world where every country walk
would be an adventure,
where every garden would become
an enchanted one...
as if a window had been opened
to let in the sun.

PRINCESS GRACE OF MONACO (1929-1982)

To lie on the grass under a tree
on a warm summer afternoon
with the scent of roses and honeysuckle
wafting on the breeze, while
iridescent blue and red dragonflies
dart across the pond and frogs lazily plop
in and out of the water-lilies,
is to be transported for a few precious hours
quite away from everyday cares.

MELANIE PHILLIPS

I spend hours in front of a computer, eyes glued
to black words and a winking black cursor.
If I drift my gaze out to the garden,
I immediately feel a change in my heartbeat,
a peaceful slowing....

RACHEL BILLINGTON, B.1942

Like the musician, the painter, the poet,
and the rest, the true lover of flowers
is born, not made. And he is born to
happiness in this vale of tears, to a certain
amount of the purest joy that earth can
give her children, joy that is tranquil,
innocent, uplifting, unfailing.
Given a little patch of ground, with time
to take care of it, with tools to work it
and seeds to plant in it, he has all he needs.

CELIA THAXTER (1835-1984)

By watching things grow, I can turn down
the noise in my brain and observe firsthand
the miracle of mindfulness.
The absolute cycle of birth, death, and renewal
displays itself before me, and I find
that I can be completely present in a way
that I never before have been….
I can allow things just to be, and with only
a helping hand from me, a large force manages
the whole game.

VIVIAN ELISABETH GLYK,
FROM "TWELVE LESSONS OF LIFE I LEARNED
FROM MY GARDEN"

The space we call a garden – whether a random grouping of plants surrounding an outdoor residential patio or an expansive, exquisitely landscaped public garden – is a non-threatening place. It's a quiet spot where we can reflect, evaluate, think, cope, and mentally restore ourselves. The garden is also a place where people can let go of their aggressions and redirect their focus and energies for positive purposes.

STEVEN H. DAVIS,
IN "MAXIMISING HUMAN POTENTIAL"

Always changing, the garden is a stimulating place
filled with excitement and discovery.
We can see the beautiful blossoms, smell
their enticing fragrance, touch their softness,
hear their brushing in a gentle breeze and,
after their flowering, even taste the fruit that follows.
The garden is a place where we can experience quiet
contemplation as well as noisy socialization,
where encouragement, confidence, self-esteem,
creativity, and a sense of accomplishment
can flower and flourish….

STEVEN H. DAVIS, IN "MAXIMISING HUMAN POTENTIAL"

In my garden there is
a large place for sentiment.
My garden of flowers
is also my garden of thoughts
and dreams.
The thoughts grow
as freely as the flowers,
and the dreams are as beautiful.

ABRAM LINWOOD URBAN

The act of pollination is the foundation upon which civilization stands.

MIRIAM WILLIAMS, FROM "ARBORETUM LEAVES"

Flowers

re like the pleasure of the world.

WILLIAM SHAKESPEARE (1564-1616)

Watching something grow
is good for morale.
It helps you believe in life.

MYRON S. KAUFMANN

We little people,
we who have signed no treaties,
painted no masterpieces,
won no great prizes –
have yet created wonders.
From time and skill
and simple things,
we have made gardens.

PAM BROWN, B.1928

Everything that slows us down
and forces patience,
everything that sets us back
into the slow cycles of nature,
is a help.
Gardening is an instrument
of grace.

MAY SARTON (1912-1995)

The garden runs through
our lives like a river through a field,
like air in our lungs.
The garden does not end in space
any more than it does in time.

MONTY DON, B.1955, FROM "MY ROOTS"

People have always dreamed of gardens.
Eden. Babylon. Gethsemane.
Paradise.
Darkness and light.
And so have fashioned gardens
from the wilderness,
places of flowers and springing water,
as signs of hope.

PAM BROWN, B.1928

Don't underestimate the therapeutic value
of gardening. It's the one area where
we can all use our nascent creative talents
to make a truly satisfying work of art.
Every individual, with thought,
patience and a large portion of help
from nature, has it in them to create
their own private paradise:
truly a thing of beauty and a joy for ever.

GEOFF HAMILTON, FROM "PARADISE GARDENS"

Just living is not enough....
One must have sunshine,
freedom, and a little flower.

HANS CHRISTIAN ANDERSEN

A city office, a crowded train,

a weary walk.

But home at last.

Supper – and life returning.

Stand at the kitchen door.

Breathe the evening air,

the scent of foliage and flowers.

Walk out into the gathering dark

and touch the cool of petals,

the gentleness of leaves.

The garden you have made.

PAM BROWN, B.1928

…in the garden or allotment
we are king or queen.
It is our piece of outdoors that lays
a real stake to the planet.
The garden is not just the grass
to be mown and the straggle
of weeds to be pulled from
between the paving,
but the sky and the rain
and the birds singing
in the bushes – our bushes.

MONTY DON, B.1955, FROM "MY ROOTS"

When the eye is trained to perceive pictorial effect, it is frequently struck by something – some combination of grouping, lighting and colour – that is seen to have that complete aspect of unity and beauty that to the artist's eye forms a picture. Such are the impressions that the artist-gardener endeavours to produce in every portion of the garden.

GERTRUDE JEKYLL (1843-1932)

Some people think, "I need a lot of money to garden. I need a lot of land. I need a lot of things." Well, you don't need those things at all. Just take one little pot and plant your first flower. To me, if someone is tending a single pot of flowers on a balcony or the front steps, that's still gardening. Whatever it takes for you to do it, you can make a garden happen.

REBECCA, IN "TENDING THE EARTH, MENDING THE SPIRIT"

A garden
is a grand teacher.
It teaches patience
and careful watchfulness;
it teaches industry
and thrift;
above all it teaches
entire trust.

GERTRUDE JEKYLL
(1843-1932)

A gardener always has hope.
The leaves have fallen, the earth is bare,
the flowers are gone, leaving mere sticks behind.
But gardeners have learned patience
and hope from long experience.
Spring lies only just below the frosted ground.

PAM BROWN, B.1928

The garden fills your soul with hope.

RACHEL, IN "TENDING THE EARTH, MENDING THE SPIRIT"

A garden can sometimes be
just like a time machine....
The smell of lavender takes me straight back
to my grandmother – it was her favourite scent.
Whenever I pick an apple,
I'm back harvesting fruit with my father.
When I touch lily of the valley,
I'm holding my wedding bouquet,
and when I see daisies,
I'm sitting in a meadow helping
my children make daisy chains.

MARY, IN "THE FRIENDSHIP BOOK
OF FRANCIS GAY 2006"

One of the most tragic things I know
about human nature is that all of us
tend to put off living. We are all dreaming of
some magical rose garden over the horizon instead
of enjoying the roses that are blooming
outside our windows today.

DALE CARNEGIE

Of all human activities,
apart from the procreation of children,
gardening is the most optimistic and hopeful.
The gardener is by definition one
who plans for and believes
and trusts in a future, whether
in the short or the longer term.

SUSAN HILL, FROM "THROUGH THE GARDEN GATE"

How impudent we are
to think these glorious patterns,
colours, shapes and scents
were made for our delectation.
They are flight paths for bees
and humming birds.
Hatcheries for frogs.
Nibbles for little creatures.
Changing rooms for caterpillars.
They enchant us
as a sideline.

PAM BROWN, B.1928

People are often addicted to what I call "secondary pleasures," such as drugs, alcohol, shopping, fast cars, movies, and so on. One reason is because they're so disconnected from the "primary pleasures," such as feeling grounded and connected to living things. We are so exiled, disconnected, and spacey in our culture. We need to acknowledge that and seek alternatives. Home is where our heart and hearth are, where we feel warm and inclusive and have a sense of belonging. Most people don't feel they belong anymore. They're disconnected from body, soul, and family. Gardening is a strategy for getting reconnected to the earth. People get rejuvenated by it.

SHEPHERD BLISS

A real gardener is not a man who cultivates flowers;
he is a man who cultivates the soil....

KAREL CAPEK (1890-1938), FROM "THE GARDENER'S YEAR"

All gardens are by people and for people.
A collection of plants, however rare and wonderful,
is only of interest to the collector.
Yet a few simple plants in old cans tended
with love and shared with friends and neighbours
can be paradise.

MONTY DON, B.1955, FROM "AROUND
THE WORLD IN 80 GARDENS"

There's nothing like the smell and texture of dirt. It helps me feel like I'm a part of my planet, of my universe. It also connects me to the billions of people who have gone before me, tending the earth for thousands of generations. We've made ourselves crazy as a society – always pushing, pushing, pushing – and gardening offers us a life after all that craziness. It's in the fiber of our being to touch the earth, to tend its plants. After all, this is our home – this is where we belong.

FROM "TENDING THE EARTH, MENDING THE SPIRIT"

…academic studies suggest
horticulture therapy may lower
blood pressure, slow bone loss,
improve circulation,
and reduce stress.

CONNIE GOLDMAN & RICHARD MAHLER

Gardening affords us a deep appreciation for the continuity of nature's seasons and cycles as well as an understanding of the interconnectedness of all living things.

Our souls are enriched in the garden by the business of helping create new life, even when things look bleak and hopeless. We come to a greater acceptance of birth, disease, and death because these are constantly being presented to us.

There is an appreciation of nature's infinite beauty and intrinsic rhythms as well. We are humbled by our gardens because they teach us that nature has its own plan, which includes us. This design is more diverse and complex than we ever can hope to understand.

RUCY, IN "TENDING THE EARTH, MENDING THE SPIRIT"

The poetry of the earth is

never dead.

JOHN KEATS, FROM "ON THE GRASSHOPPER AND THE CRICKET"

Gardening is a long road,
with many detours and way stations,
and here we all are at one point or another.
It's not a question of superior or
inferior taste, merely a question of
which detour we are on at the moment.
Getting there (as they say) is not important;
the wandering about in the wilderness
or in the olive groves or in the bayous
is the whole point.

HENRY MITCHELL, FROM "GARDENING IS A LONG ROAD"

Now I see the secret of making
the best persons. It is to grow in the open air,
and to eat and sleep with the earth.

WALT WHITMAN, FROM "LEAVES OF GRASS"

Like the fruits, when cooler weather
and frosts arrive, we too are braced
and ripened. When we shift from
the shady to the sunny side of the house,
and sit there in an extra coat for warmth,
our green and leafy and pulpy thoughts
acquire colour and flavour,
and perchance a sweet nuttiness at last,
worth your cracking.

HENRY DAVID THOREAU

When I sit next to my potted plants,
I feel like I'm in touch with eternity,
with something that goes on and on.
I really love that feeling of being
fundamentally connected to the cycles
of life and of nature.

KATE, IN "TENDING THE EARTH,
MENDING THE SPIRIT"

All gardens have the potential to be sensuous,
poetic places, feeding the soul as well as
letting us spread beyond the house....
There is something happening there that goes
beyond horticulture just as a superb loaf
of bread or bottle of wine goes beyond nutrition.
In a world of terror and anxiety this is art
in a million backyards. There is a real sense
that in making your garden "better"
according to your own taste,
then you are doing more than outdoor decorating.
I absolutely believe that you are making
the world a better place for everyone else as well.

MONTY DON, B.1955, FROM "MY ROOTS"

The soul cannot thrive
in the absence of a garden.
If you don't want paradise,
you are not human;
and if you are not human
you don't have a soul.

THOMAS MOORE,
FROM "THE RE-ENCHANTMENT
OF EVERYDAY LIFE"

I get energy from the earth itself,
and I get optimism from the earth itself.
I feel that as long as the earth can make
a spring every year, I can.
As long as the earth can flower
and produce nurturing fruit,
I can, because I'm the earth.
I won't give up until the earth gives up.

ALICE WALKER, B.1944

Our modern world is principally composed
of straight lines, solid flat surfaces and the sharp points
of right angles. In the garden you find curves,
few flat surfaces, far more rounded effects.
You are in a place that is no longer hard on the eyes.
Most people feel pretty powerless in the face
of what is going on around them, but each of us
does have control of a small part of the planet
that we can make a little greener,
more full of wildlife and leave a more fruitful place
than when we found it.

BOB FLOWERDEW, FROM "TELEGRAPH MAGAZINE", 2003

If we are to survive as a species
and preserve the environment
on our troubled planet, we must
claim, celebrate, and protect our
precious bond with nature.
We can do this in our gardens.

CONNIE GOLDMAN & RICHARD MAHLER

If you love this book...

...look out for other Helen Exley Giftbooks. There are over 300 thoughtful gift ideas listed on our website. There is something for mothers, daughters and other members of the family, and for friends. There are also important titles on wisdom, values and calm. Here are just four titles on gardens and personal peace:

My Little Garden Book
(also edited by Dalton Exley)
And Wisdom Comes Quietly
Taking Time to Just Be
The Little Green Book
(on over 100 actions
to help the environment)

And a few of our other top books:
To a very special Mother
Wisdom For Our Times
Timeless Values
Go Girl!
A Friend... (Jewel)
A Gift of Happiness (Jewel)
This Too Will Pass

What is a Helen Exley Giftbook?

Helen Exley Giftbooks cover the most powerful range of all human relationships: love between couples, the bonds within families and between friends, and the themes of personal values and wisdom. No expense is spared in making sure that each book is as thoughtful and meaningful a gift as it is possible to create: good to give, good to receive. You have the result in your hands. If you have loved it – please tell others! There is no power on earth like the word-of-mouth recommendation of friends!

Helen Exley Giftbooks
16 Chalk Hill,
Watford, Herts,
WD19 4BG, UK.

Visit Helen Exley's website to see the full list of titles:
www.helenexleygiftbooks.com

ACKNOWLEDGEMENTS:
The publishers are grateful for permission to reproduce copyright material. Whilst every effort has been made to trace copyright holders, the publishers would be pleased to hear from any not here acknowledged.

DAN BARKER: from *Chicken Soup for the Gardener's Soul* by Dan Barker, founder of The Home Gardening Project Foundation.

GEOFFREY B. CHARLESWORTH: from *The Opinionated Gardener* by Geoffrey B. Charlesworth, reprinted by permission of David R. Godine, Publisher, Inc. Copyright © 1988 by Geoffrey B. Charlesworth.

BOB FLOWERDEW: from *The Telegraph Magazine*, 2003, with kind permission from Bob Flowerdew www.bobflowerdew.co.uk

CONNIE GOLDMAN and RICHARD MAHLER: Quotes from *Tending the Earth, Mending the Spirit: Healing Gifts of Gardening*, copyright © 2006 by Connie Goldman and Richard Mahler, used by the authors' permission. Learn more about their work at www.richardmahler.com and www.congoldman.org.

DANIEL J. HINKLEY: from *The Explorer's Garden: Rare and Unusual Plant*, with kind permission from Daniel J. Hinkley.

KETZEL LEVINE: author of *Plant This!*

KENT NERBURN: excerpted from *Small Graces: The Quiet Gifts of Everyday Life* by Kent Nerburn, published by New World Library. Visit the author's website at www.kentnerburn.com

ROY STRONG: From *Garden Party* by Roy Strong published by Frances Lincoln Ltd, copyright © 2000. Reproduced by permission of Frances Lincoln Ltd.

LIST OF ILLUSTRATIONS:
Cover, Title Page and Endpapers: Photography by Richard Exley © Exley Creative Ltd.

Pages 6, 9, 15, 20, 22, 25, 27, 29, 31, 32-33, 36, 38-39, 42, 44, 46, 48, 50, 57, 61, 64, 66-67, 68-69, 73, 80, 84, 89, 90, 92, 94, 96-97, 98, 100, 113, 114-115, 126, 129, 130-131, 134-135: Photography by Richard Exley © Exley Creative Ltd.

Pages 11, 35, 83, 106, 120: Derek Harris/The Garden Collection

Page 12: Nicola Stocken Tomkins/The Garden Collection.

Pages 16-17, 86: Gary Rogers/The Garden Collection – Design: Tom Stuart Smith

Page 18: Derek St Romaine/The Garden Collection

Page 41: Andrew Lawson/The Garden Collection

Page 52: Jonathan Buckley/The Garden Collection – Design: Gay Wilson

Page 55: Marie O'Hara/The Garden Collection – Design: Denise Preston

Page 59: Jonathan Buckley/The Garden Design: Diarmud Gavin

Pages 63, 139: Derek Harris/The Garden Collection – La Plessis Sasnieres

Page 71: Neil Sutherland/The Garden Collection

Pages 74, 133: Gary Rogers/The Garden Collection

Page 77: Andrew Lawson/The Garden Collection – Beth Chatto Gardens

Page 79: Steven Wooster/The Garden Collection – Beth Chatto Gardens

Page 102: Jonathan Buckley/The Garden Collection – Design: Helen Yemm

Page 104-105: Gary Rogers/The Garden Collection – Design: Mr & Mrs Cesare Settepassi

Page 108: Torie Chugg/The Garden Collection

Page 110: Jonathan Buckley/The Garden Collection – Design: Virginia Kennedy

Page 116: Jonathan Buckley/The Garden Collection – Design: Christopher Lloyd

People are always asking,
"What is the purpose of life?"
That's easy.
Relieve suffering.
Create beauty. Make gardens.

DAN BARKER,
IN "CHICKEN SOUP FOR THE GARDENER'S SOUL"

There is something about a garden
that is so much bigger than oneself.
I am left with a great feeling of trust,
knowing that nature and its life force
will continue long after I'm gone.

FROM "TENDING THE EARTH,
MENDING THE SPIRIT"

Life, death, earth and sky all come together
in the intimacy of a garden's space.
It is a metaphor too rich to exhaust, a perfect
microcosm of the universe's deepest wisdom,
a constant reminder that we must accept the
forces of nature if we are to survive.

KENT NERBURN, B.1946, FROM "SMALL GRACES"